Americans All biographies are inspiring life stories about people of all races, creeds, and nationalities who have uniquely contributed to the American way of life. Highlights from each person's story develop his contributions in his special field — whether they be in the arts, industry, human rights, education, science and medicine, or sports.

Specific abilities, character, and accomplishments are emphasized. Often despite great odds, these famous people have attained success in their fields through the good use of ability, determination, and hard work. These fast-moving stories of real people will show the way to better understanding of the ingredients necessary for personal success.

Grandma
Moses

FAVORITE PAINTER

by Charles P. Graves

illustrated by Victor Mays

GARRARD PUBLISHING COMPANY
CHAMPAIGN, ILLINOIS

*For those painting soldiers of the
10th Mountain Division, John Fitzgerald
and Robert Wheeler*

Acknowledgments:

Grandma Moses: My Life's History, edited by Otto Kallir, copyright by Grandma Moses Properties, Inc., and published by Harper & Row, was a primary source for much of the material in this book.

The author wishes to thank Mr. and Mrs. Loyd Moses, Mr. and Mrs. Forrest Moses, Mrs. Hugh Moses and Dr. Otto Kallir for reading the manuscript and making many suggestions.

Picture credits:

All paintings by Grandma Moses and portraits of the artist: © Copyright Grandma Moses Properties, Inc., New York City. All photographs: Courtesy of The Galerie St. Etienne, New York

p. 52: Webb Gallery of American Art, Shelburne Museum, Shelburne, Vermont

p. 85: From *The Night Before Christmas* by Clement C. Moore, with illustrations by Grandma Moses. Reproduced by permission of Random House, Inc. © Copyright 1960 and 1961 by Grandma Moses Properties, Inc., New York City

Contents

1. Triumph and Tragedy 7

2. Sugaring Off 12

3. Hired Girl 21

4. Virginia 29

5. Eagle Bridge 41

6. Starting to Paint Again 50

7. Anna Mary Becomes
   Grandma Moses 58

8. Grandma Goes to Washington . . 68

9. Grandma on TV 76

10. A Painting for a President 83

11. One Hundred Years Young 88

1. Triumph and Tragedy

On an April day in 1865, Anna Mary Robertson looked out the window and saw her father rein in his horse and leap to the ground. He flung open the front door and shouted, "I've got wonderful news! Robert E. Lee has surrendered to General Grant! The war is almost over!"

As Anna Mary was only four and one-half years old she could not understand all that the Union victory meant. But she was glad the Civil War was ending.

Anna Mary lived with her family on a farm near Greenwich, a town in upstate New York close to the Vermont border. She had three brothers: Lester, nine; Horace, seven; and Arthur, three.

"Anna Mary," Mr. Robertson said later, "tell the boys to get some cowbells from the barn for noisemakers. We'll all go to Greenwich to celebrate Grant's victory."

The Robertsons piled into the buggy and rode to Greenwich. Church bells were ringing, whistles were blowing, and people were shouting.

Anna Mary and her brothers jumped from the buggy to join the other children racing up and down Main Street.

"Hooray for General Grant!" the children cried. "Three cheers for President

Anna Mary at
the age of four

Lincoln!" Anna Mary rang her cowbells
with all her might.

A few days later Mrs. Robertson took
Anna Mary to visit her grandmother in
Eagle Bridge, south of Greenwich. In a
town on the way, Mrs. Robertson noticed
that people were draping their houses with
black crepe.

"Something just terrible must have happened," she said.

10

Mrs. Robertson stopped the buggy in front of a store. "I'm going to find out what's wrong," she said.

When she returned to the buggy, tears were splashing down her cheeks.

"What's the matter, Ma?" Anna Mary asked.

"President Lincoln is dead," sobbed Mrs. Robertson. "He was shot last night and died early today."

Although she was only a small child, the tragedy made a great impression on Anna Mary. When she became famous as Grandma Moses, she often talked about the day Lincoln died.

2. Sugaring Off

"I dreamed about you last night, Anna Mary," Mr. Robertson said one morning after his daughter's fifth birthday. "I was in a big hall crowded with people. They were clapping and cheering to beat the band. Suddenly I saw you walking toward me on the shoulders of the people. It was *you* they were cheering."

"What does the dream mean, Pa?" Anna Mary asked.

"Who knows what dreams mean!" her father exclaimed. "Maybe it means that someday you'll be famous.

When Anna Mary was six, she started going to school with her older brothers. Though Anna Mary was hardly bigger than an imp, she thought she could do anything her brothers could do. She often raced them to school, and sometimes she won. She hated to be beaten at anything.

At school all the grades were taugnt in the same room. Anna Mary was poor at spelling, but she learned to read quickly.

She also learned many useful things at home. Her mother taught her to churn butter, to make candles and soap, and to sew. Anna Mary's father was proud of her. One day when he was leaving for Greenwich, Anna Mary begged him to buy her some candy.

"I'll bring you a present," he promised, "but it won't be candy."

When he returned, Mr. Robertson gave all the children big sheets of the kind of paper that newspapers are printed on.

"Now draw some nice pictures," he said. "Pictures last longer than candy."

Anna Mary shut her eyes and imagined the view from her front porch. Then she drew a picture of the hills which rolled in the distance. She had only one piece of blue chalk.

"I know hills are green," Anna Mary told her father. "But I don't have any green chalk."

"That's all right," he said. "From a distance hills do look blue, except when they're covered with snow."

When all her paper and chalk were used up, Anna Mary got some red paint from the barn and started painting a picture on a piece of wood.

"What are you painting, Anna Mary?" her brother Lester asked.

"A *lambscape*," Anna Mary said.

Lester laughed and corrected her. "You mean *landscape*."

"No I don't," Anna Mary insisted. "This is the paint that Pa uses for marking the lambs. So I'm painting a lambscape."

"You're using only one color," Lester said.

"Red is the only color I have."

"Let's make some paint," Lester suggested, "out of berries."

The children went out in the fields and picked blueberries and elderberries. They used the juices for paint. Anna Mary liked her pictures, and she showed them to her parents.

"You're wasting your time," her mother told her. "You should be doing practical things."

Anna Mary started to cry aloud, but her father patted her. "Your pictures are pretty," he said.

Mr. Robertson liked to paint too. When Mrs. Robertson asked him to paint the walls of one of the rooms, he decorated them with beautiful mountain scenes.

But Mr. Robertson didn't have much time to paint. Nearly every year a new baby arrived, and he had to work harder than ever to feed his growing family. The next three children after Arthur were girls, and Anna Mary was delighted to have sisters. She helped her mother with the many farm chores, and she often took care of the younger children.

In early spring, the Robertsons always

17

made sugar from the sap of the sugar
maples on their land.

"How soon is sugaring-off time, Pa?"
Anna Mary asked one morning at breakfast.

"The thermometer reads 40 degrees,"
Mr. Robertson said. "That's just right,
so we'll start today." The temperature

had to be above freezing for the sap to
flow. Mr. Robertson bored holes in the
sugar maples and attached metal cups to
catch the sap.

Early the next morning Anna Mary
and the other children ran from tree to
tree, collecting the sap in buckets. Mr.
Robertson built a fire in the backyard and

placed a huge kettle over it. The children emptied their buckets into the kettle.

Late that afternoon it began to snow. "Hooray!" Anna Mary shouted. "Now we'll have maple sugar candy!"

When the ground was white, Anna Mary dipped a spoon in the kettle and filled it with the sap, which had boiled down until it was thick. She dropped the sap on the snow, and it quickly hardened into candy.

"Maybe candy doesn't last as long as pictures," Anna Mary told her father with a grin. "But it sure tastes a whole lot better than paint."

3. Hired Girl

Early one evening an elderly couple named Mr. and Mrs. Thomas Whiteside came to the Robertson farm. They were distant relatives.

"I'm getting too old to do housework," Mrs. Whiteside said. "We're looking for a hired girl."

"Anna Mary would make a good house-keeper," Mrs. Robertson suggested. "She has more energy than a bumblebee."

"But she's only twelve and small for her age," Mr. Robertson objected. "She should stay in school."

Schooling for girls was not considered important in those days. "It won't hurt her to miss this year," Mrs. Robertson argued. "And Anna Mary will learn a lot about housekeeping with the Whitesides." Finally Mr. Robertson agreed to let Anna Mary take the job. The Whitesides lived nearby and she could see her family often.

Anna Mary was excited about leaving home, but she was also nervous. She had heard that the Whitesides' big house was haunted.

Anna Mary shuddered on her first night there when she blew out her candle and crawled into bed. The moon, shining through the tree outside her window, made eerie patterns on the walls.

"I don't believe in ghosts," Anna Mary tried to tell herself. Just then a window rattled. Anna Mary pulled the covers over her head. The next thing she knew the sun was shining in her window.

Mr. and Mrs. Whiteside were friendly and kind. Anna Mary tried hard to please them. She did all the washing and ironing and cooked three meals a day.

"I'm only twelve years old," she thought proudly, "and yet I can do the work of a grownup."

Instead of returning to school, Anna Mary stayed with the Whitesides for four years. Then she started to work for a woman in Eagle Bridge.

"You must go back to school," her new mistress said. "You can do housework after your classes." Anna Mary gladly returned to school.

At fifteen, Anna Mary was a hired girl at the Whiteside farm.

Her favorite subject was geography, because it gave her a chance to draw. One of her assignments was to draw a map of North America. Instead of just writing the mountains' names, Anna Mary drew pictures of towering peaks covered with trees and rocks and snow.

25

When Anna Mary was seventeen, she was hired by Mrs. David Burch, who lived close to the town of Cambridge. One of Anna Mary's duties was to draw water from the well in a big oaken bucket.

"Do you know the song called *The Old Oaken Bucket*?" Mrs. Burch asked her one day.

"The old oaken bucket," Anna Mary sang, "the ironbound bucket, the moss-covered bucket that hung in the well."

"Let me tell you the story about that song," Mrs. Burch began. "The original old oaken bucket used to hang right in this well," Mrs. Burch told her. "A great-great-uncle of mine named Paul Dennis, who grew up on this farm, used to fetch water in it. He fell in love with a girl who lived nearby. Her parents did not like him. They broke up the romance."

"What did Paul do?" Anna Mary asked.

"He went to sea for three years," Mrs. Burch replied, "to try to forget the girl. He forgot the girl, but he was so homesick for the family farm that he wrote a poem about the old oaken bucket hanging here. He gave the poem to a man called Samuel Woodworth. Woodworth changed some of the words and published it early in this century."

"Is that really true?" Anna Mary asked.

"I can't prove it," Mrs. Burch admitted. "But it's a good story."

"I like it too," Anna Mary agreed.

When Anna Mary was 27, she met a hired man named Thomas Salmon Moses. She thought he was the most handsome man she had ever seen. Like Anna Mary, he loved to work, and could do almost everything. She respected him because he was always helping other people. Anna Mary and Thomas became great friends.

"I'd like to move to the South," Thomas said to Anna Mary one day.

"What would you do down there?" Anna Mary asked.

"I've had an offer of a job on a horse farm in North Carolina."

"Are you going to take it?" Anna Mary looked worried.

"I might look it over," Thomas said, "if you will go with me—as my wife."

So Anna Mary and Thomas became engaged and were married soon afterward.

"You are taking away the nicest girl in upstate New York," one of Thomas' friends said as the young couple boarded the train and started for North Carolina.

4. Virginia

On their way to North Carolina, Anna
Mary and Thomas Moses changed trains
in Washington, D. C. They got aboard
the wrong train and found themselves in
the western part of Virginia.

"This is such beautiful country that I'm
glad we did make a mistake," Anna Mary
said, laughing.

The next day Anna Mary and Thomas
started for North Carolina again. As the
train chugged through the Shenandoah
Valley, Anna Mary gazed in wonder out

of the window. She could hardly take her eyes off the beautiful Blue Ridge Mountains. If only she could paint them!

When their train reached Staunton, Virginia, Anna Mary said, "Mercy me, I'm tired. Let's stay here for the weekend."

Thomas agreed. The "weekend" lasted for eighteen years. Instead of going on to North Carolina, they rented a 100-acre farm in Virginia's Shenandoah Valley. After buying two cows and some horses and chickens, Anna Mary and Thomas Moses went to work.

Anna Mary started churning butter. She made much more than she and her husband could use.

"What are you going to do with all that butter?" a neighbor asked.

"I'm going to ask Thomas to sell it to a grocery store," she replied.

"They won't pay you but eight cents a pound," the neighbor objected.

Thomas took a few pounds of the butter to a Staunton store. The owner tasted it and exclaimed, "Gee, it's great! I can't pay you in cash, but I'll allow you twelve cents a pound in trade."

Thomas traded the butter for sugar. A few days later the grocer sent them word that Anna Mary's butter was so popular he would pay 20 cents a pound in cash.

Anna Mary was pleased. Soon she made as much money as the cows originally cost.

One morning the grocer's brother came to the Moses farm. "Your butter is wonderful," he told Anna Mary. "Nobody here can make butter so well."

The man said he had a 600-acre farm

north of Staunton. "If you rent my farm, you can make your butter in larger quantities. I will give you 50 cents a pound for all the butter you can make," he proposed.

"I don't know," Thomas shook his head. "My wife is expecting a baby. Maybe we shouldn't move."

"Why, Thomas!" Anna Mary exclaimed. "Fifty cents a pound is a heap of money. We can't afford *not* to move."

They moved to the larger farm, bought a herd of dairy cows, and started making even more butter. As Anna Mary churned the butter, she often looked out the window at the beautiful Shenandoah Valley and the Blue Ridge Mountains.

"Oh, how I wish I had time to paint again," Anna Mary said to herself. But there was never enough time.

Anna Mary and her two youngest children,
Anna and Hugh, about 1904

Soon Anna Mary was busier than ever,
taking care of a baby daughter, Winona.
Three years after Winona's birth, a son,
Loyd, was born. While the two children
were still almost babies, Anna Mary and
Thomas moved to an even larger dairy
farm. Their house, made of brick, was
three stories high.

34

On their new farm Anna Mary and Thomas made their living selling milk. Anna Mary washed a hundred milk bottles a day, but she was never too busy to play with her children. A year and a half after Loyd was born she had another son, Forrest.

Later two more children arrived, Anna and Hugh. With five lively children about, something exciting was always happening on the farm.

One day Anna Mary heard a knock on the door. When she opened it, a man about her own age was standing there.

"Good morning," the man said. "I'm looking for work. Do you need a hired man?"

"My husband used to be a hired man," Anna Mary told him. "A hired man has to work mighty hard."

"I'm not afraid of work," the man said.

"Well, what is your name?" Anna Mary asked.

"Andy."

"Andy what?"

"Just Andy," the man answered. "You see, I was born a slave, and slaves didn't have last names. I was about three years old when the Civil War ended and I was freed."

"How would you like to be called Andy Moses?" Anna Mary asked. "Then if you get any mail, the postman will know to bring it here."

"That's fine with me," the man said.

So, as Andy Moses, the new hired man moved into the house. He helped plow the fields, plant the crops, and tend the livestock. In his own horse and buggy, he often took the Moses children for rides.

And when the children were sick, Andy took care of them.

"I don't know what the children would do without you, Andy," Anna Mary told him.

The Moses children didn't have many toys, but they certainly had a lot of fun. On birthdays their mother always baked a big cake, with one layer for each year of the birthday child's age.

When Winona was eleven, Anna Mary decided to stop adding a new layer on each birthday.

"By the time you reach one hundred," she said, "the cake would be more than ten feet high."

Though she stopped adding a layer each year, the decorations on the birthday cakes were always works of art. Anna Mary painted pictures with icing, making the most beautiful cakes the children had ever seen.

Anna Mary always made the family's Christmas tree a work of art too. She and the children decorated it with strings of popcorn and colored paper. Golden oranges were tied to the branches, as well as simple presents such as pocket knives and combs.

One Christmas Eve when Anna Mary had just finished making a batch of ginger cookies, she heard bells ringing outside. She went to the door and saw a man wearing cow horns on his head. Children from all over the countryside were following him. The man told Anna Mary that he was Santa Claus.

"You look more like the Pied Piper to me," Anna Mary said, looking at his followers. "But come in and have some

Christmas cookies and bring all the children with you."

Every Christmas morning there was a hobby horse beneath the Moses tree. It was the same present the children had been given the Christmas before, and the Christmas before that.

Each December Thomas repainted the hobby horse until it gleamed like new. He always made a new tail from one of Anna Mary's hair switches.

The children knew that their mother and father couldn't afford expensive gifts. When they saw the hobby horse beneath the tree, they always acted surprised in order to make their parents happy.

5. Eagle Bridge

In 1905 Anna Mary and Thomas Moses decided to return to New York. They bought a dairy farm near Eagle Bridge, where they would be close to Anna's brothers and sisters. They hired a whole freight car to transport their possessions. Besides their furniture, they would take their cows, their chickens, and their dog.

"Somebody has to ride in the freight car to take care of the animals," Anna Mary said.

"I guess that somebody had better be me," her husband remarked. "Loyd and Forrest can go with me to help." Loyd

was fourteen now, and Forrest was twelve.

Anna Mary fixed a bed for the boys in the freight car and tied down a kerosene stove so it wouldn't tip over.

The girls, little Hugh, and Anna Mary boarded a passenger train. They reached Eagle Bridge two days ahead of the others. When the freight car arrived, Anna Mary went to meet her husband and the boys.

"How was the trip?" she asked.

"It was fun," Forrest said. "It was a camping trip on wheels."

Anna Mary's brothers and sisters helped the Moses family get settled in their new home. Anna Mary and Thomas bought more dairy cows and began to sell milk.

Every morning Anna Mary got up before dawn, fed the chickens and fixed a hearty breakfast for her large family.

She washed clothes, baked bread, sewed, worked in her garden, and, of course, took care of her children. She let the children have more fun than many mothers did, in those times.

One day when one of their aunts was visiting, the children had a water fight. As they finished dinner, Loyd suddenly threw a glass of water at Forrest. Then Forrest threw water on Winona. With shouts of glee young Anna and Hugh joined the fray.

The children ran outdoors to the pump. They filled buckets with water and soaked each other, roaring with laughter.

Their aunt said to Anna Mary, "I would not stand for this."

"Land sakes, they're having fun!" Anna Mary exclaimed. "And they're only young once. Let them enjoy being young!"

But Anna Mary could hardly believe how fast her children were growing up. One after another, they finished school, got married, and moved out of the house, until only Hugh was left. When Hugh was nineteen, he married a lovely girl named Dorothy Harrison.

"Why don't you and Dorothy live with us?" Anna Mary asked her youngest son. "We have lots of room, and we'd be lonesome with all our children gone."

After their wedding trip Dorothy and Hugh made their home with Anna Mary and Thomas. Dorothy had never lived on a farm before, but she soon learned how to bake bread, preserve vegetables, and do the other household tasks.

Thanks to Dorothy, Anna Mary had more leisure time now. She started to paint. Some of her sisters had taken

painting lessons, but Anna Mary had never taken a lesson in her life.

At first Thomas didn't think much of her pictures. Then one night he pointed to a painting. "Who did that?" he asked. "It's good."

"If it's good, one of my sisters must have painted it," Anna Mary said. Then

47

she saw that the picture was one of hers. She felt pleased with herself and with her husband. After that Thomas often sat and watched while she painted.

Once Anna Mary painted a picture on the fire screen in the living room. First she pasted a piece of paper over the screen and painted it a solid color. Then she painted in two trees and a lake.

Dorothy's grandfather came to visit soon after Anna Mary finished the painting.

"Oh, isn't that beautiful!" he exclaimed. "That's the most wonderful picture I have ever seen." Anna Mary blushed with pride. She was happy when people praised her pictures. Thomas was as pleased by the compliments as if he'd done the paintings himself.

Although he was in his sixties, Thomas still worked hard on the farm. One cold day in January, 1927, he went out in a blizzard to get some wood.

"I'm so cold," he said, when he came back to the house.

Anna Mary made him sit by the fire and brought him a cup of hot tea. Soon she heard him choking and realized he was sick.

She had no telephone, so Hugh went to a neighbor's house to call Dr. Clayton Shaw, the family doctor.

Before Dr. Shaw could get there, Thomas Moses died of a heart attack.

"Even if I had been here," Dr. Shaw told the weeping Anna Mary, "I could not have saved him."

6. Starting to Paint Again

Although she missed Thomas, Anna Mary Moses was never lonesome for long. She often visited her children and grandchildren.

Her youngest daughter, Anna, who had two children, lived in nearby Vermont. Once while Mrs. Moses was there, her daughter said, "Mother, I wish you would make me a yarn picture. I saw one recently that was very pretty, but I know you could make a better one."

"What makes you think I could do one at all?" her mother asked.

"You can do everything," young Anna said. "Anyone who can sew and knit and paint as well as you do, can make a yarn picture."

A yarn picture is a scene stitched on a piece of cloth, in wool of various colors. Anna Mary went to work and soon produced a beautiful picture.

Her daughter loved it, and many other people admired it. Anna Mary made many yarn pictures and gave them away as presents. She enjoyed her new hobby.

However, as Anna Mary grew older, she developed arthritis in her hands. The joints of her fingers became stiff and caused her great pain when she stitched.

"I want to keep busy," she said to one of her sisters, "but my fingers ache terribly when I use a needle."

"It should be easier to hold a paint

"Christmas at Home" (1946)

brush," her sister suggested. "Why not
go back to painting?"

"Why that's a good idea," Anna Mary
agreed. "And moths don't eat paint."

So Anna Mary started to paint with
real purpose. Before she began a picture,
she would shut her eyes and imagine a
scene from her childhood. Her pictures

"The Mailman Has Gone" (1949)

contained red barns and white houses, horse-drawn sleighs, church steeples, and miles and miles of snow. They had no telephone poles, no mail boxes, no fire hydrants. But they had lots of horses, cows, chickens, and children. Anna Mary loved people so much that she often put too many of them in her pictures.

"I see the whole picture before I begin to paint," she said. "It's all imagination. I paint what I remember." One thing she remembered vividly from her childhood was sugaring off. She painted many pictures about making sugar from the maples.

Soon after she started painting, she entered some pictures in a county fair. She

"Sugaring Off" (About 1940)

also entered some homemade raspberry jam. Her jam won a prize, but her pictures were hardly noticed.

Most people who did notice her pictures loved them. Anna Mary gave away many pictures as presents, and sometimes she sold one for a few dollars.

Her son Hugh and his wife, Dorothy, were especially enthusiastic about her pictures. Anna Mary called Hugh her "art critic." One day soon after her 78th birthday, they took several of the best paintings and put them on display at Thomas' Drug Store in Hoosick Falls.

A short time later Anna Mary came home from a visit with a friend to find Dorothy tremendously excited.

"While you were away, a man came to see you," Dorothy reported breathlessly. "He said he wants to buy *all* your pictures.

He's already bought those at Thomas' Drug Store."

"Land sakes, that's exciting news," Anna Mary said. "What's the man's name?"

"Louis J. Caldor," Dorothy replied. "He's an art collector from New York City. He's coming back tomorrow to see your other paintings. I told him you had ten."

"I have only nine," Anna Mary said. "But I have a big one I can cut in two."

Anna Mary stayed up late that night cutting the picture in half and putting the two parts in separate frames.

Early the next day Mr. Caldor arrived. Anna Mary showed him her ten paintings, and he was delighted. He bought them all for three or four dollars each.

"These pictures are just beautiful," Mr. Caldor said as he put them in his car. "You certainly must love to paint."

"I like to paint old-timey things—things that are pretty," Anna Mary answered. "Most of my paintings are dreams of the past."

"Well, I certainly hope you will continue painting your dreams," Mr. Caldor said. "You will hear from me again."

7. Anna Mary Becomes *Grandma Moses*

A year later, in the fall of 1939, Anna Mary heard from Mr. Caldor that three of her paintings had been accepted for showing at the Museum of Modern Art in New York.

The show was called "Contemporary Unknown American Painters." Anna Mary's paintings were hung in the museum for a month, but they did not attract much attention. After the show was over, Anna Mary Moses was still a contemporary unknown American painter.

But Mr. Caldor believed that she was a fine artist. He returned to Eagle Bridge several times, bought more of Anna Mary's colorful pictures, and took them back to New York.

He showed the pictures to many New York art dealers, but none seemed interested. They thought Anna Mary was just an ordinary example of what they called a "primitive artist," that is, a decorative but simple painter with no training. They saw no distinctive ability in her work.

Finally Mr. Caldor heard about an art dealer who had just moved to America from Europe and had opened an art gallery in New York. The dealer, Dr. Otto Kallir, had long been interested in folk art and was well known as an expert on primitive paintings.

Mr. Caldor showed Dr. Kallir examples of Anna Mary's work. Dr. Kallir did not like all the paintings, but he was delighted with some of them.

"The paintings were done in a childlike way," he said later, "yet they had great sincerity and vitality. Anna Mary may paint like a child, but she paints like one child in a million." He preferred to call Anna Mary a "natural" painter rather than a "primitive."

Dr. Kallir decided to show some of Anna Mary's paintings in his gallery, the Galerie St. Etienne. He invited her to come to the showing.

She declined, explaining that she was too busy hanging wallpaper and putting up preserves to go to New York just then.

Dr. Kallir called Anna Mary's show "What a Farm Wife Painted." Just before it opened, a story about it appeared in the New York *Herald Tribune*. The headline read:

GRANDMA MOSES, UNTAUGHT
UPSTATE ARTIST, TO SHOW
WORKS AT A CITY GALLERY

This was the first time Anna Mary had been called "Grandma Moses" in print. Other newspapers started writing stories about her and using the nickname, and people forgot that her first name was Anna Mary.

Though Grandma Moses did not attend her first show, many art lovers did. The show was particularly popular with elderly people, who were glad to see pictures that reminded them of their childhood years.

Still the show was not an overwhelming

success. The art critic of *The New York Times* reported that "Mrs. Moses has kept to a sense of proportion, has kept her pictures small and has produced simple decorative effects . . . . This is a very creditable show of its kind." Not bad, but not very good either.

Dr. Kallir, however, was convinced that the more Grandma Moses' paintings were seen, the more popular they would become. Soon after her show at the gallery closed, he arranged for her paintings to be displayed in the exhibition hall of Gimbels department store.

Grandma Moses had time to visit New York for the Gimbels show. She attracted attention wherever she went. Newspaper reporters were delighted by her good humor and common sense, while photographers thought she looked like the ideal grandmother. They loved taking Grandma's picture.

"If people want to make a fuss over me," she said, "I don't mind. But I was the same person before I started painting as I am now."

At Gimbels she gave a short talk to several hundred people. As she finished,

Grandma's "Turkey in the Straw" was one of the early paintings shown at Gimbels.

someone took her arm to help her off the speakers' platform.

"Land sakes," she said with a grin, "at home I've been working on a ladder hanging wallpaper, and in New York you don't think I can step a few inches without help."

Although she was eighty years old, Grandma Moses was as spry as a sparrow. She stood only slightly more than five feet tall and weighed less than a hundred pounds. But she walked briskly and sparkled with the joy of being alive.

The next spring Grandma Moses entered a painting in the New York State Fair at Syracuse. Before she painted it, she had shut her eyes to remember the well on Mrs. Burch's farm. She called it "The Old Oaken Bucket." It won a prize of $250 at the fair.

"The Old Automobile" of Grandma's memory became one of her best-loved paintings.

Slowly at first, and then faster and faster, not only art lovers, but also museums started to buy Grandma Moses' paintings. As she gained more experience, the quality of her work improved. Millions of people, whether they knew much or little about art, fell in love with her pictures. They fell in love with Grandma Moses too.

They were delighted that an ordinary housewife could begin painting at eighty and be a success. Many elderly men and women felt encouraged to try painting, too.

Dr. Kallir became her representative; later he established a company called Grandma Moses Properties, Inc., which was authorized to choose and print reproductions from her paintings. As an art expert, he gave Grandma Moses good advice, but she didn't always take it.

She liked to put "glitter" on her snow scenes. But Dr. Kallir disapproved, as he thought the "glitter" cheapened her work.

"Have you ever been in the country on a sunny winter day?" she asked him. "You would see how the sun shines on the snow and makes it sparkle all over." Dr. Kallir had to give in.

With the help of Dr. Kallir, Grandma Moses began to make money, but at first it didn't mean much to her. Once he sent her a check for several thousand dollars. Weeks went by and she didn't cash it. Dr. Kallir told her the bank might not honor the check unless she cashed it within three months.

Then Grandma Moses cashed the check, brought the money home, and started giving it away to her relatives and friends.

8. Grandma Goes to Washington

"Bless goodness," Grandma Moses exclaimed to some visitors one day when she was eighty-five years old, "all this fuss just because I turned artist! I'm getting fans just like a movie actor, and maybe I should get stuck up."

It was plain that she wasn't stuck up at all. She always found time to welcome the strangers who came to her house. She liked having visitors.

One of her regular visitors was Dr. Shaw. He came to see her about once a week. Grandma Moses had known him since he was a baby and she was a teenager. They were great friends.

"You ought to drink some sherry wine," Dr. Shaw said to her one day. "It will pep you up."

"Pep me up!" Grandma cried. "I feel so bright that I'm going upstairs right now and paint another picture. And when I get tired of painting, I'm going to take piano lessons."

In 1949 Grandma Moses was one of five American women selected to receive an achievement award from the Women's National Press Club in Washington, D. C.

Accompanied by her daughter-in-law, Dorothy, she stopped in New York on her way to Washington. She wore a black straw bonnet with a bow tied beneath her chin.

Cheerful as a cricket, she charmed the newspaper reporters who came to interview her.

"It's very nice to be here, but the city doesn't appeal to me," she told them.

"As picture material?" a reporter asked.

"As any material," she answered. "I prefer the song of the bird to the honk of the horn. And I like happy things to look at and to paint. Trees are prettier than skyscrapers."

"Have you any advice to give people who want to paint?" she was asked.

"Anybody can paint who wants to," she replied. "Like all kinds of work, the more you do, the better you do."

The Women's National Press Club dinner in Washington was held at a hotel. Among the other award winners was Mrs. Franklin D. Roosevelt, who was almost

a foot taller than Grandma Moses. As
Mrs. Roosevelt came up to greet her, the
little old lady popped out of her chair
and stuck out her hand.

"Land sakes," she said to the former
First Lady, "I need stilts to stand next
to you."

72

"Not at all, Grandma," Mrs. Roosevelt said. "I'll stoop down and be on your level."

The next day Grandma Moses was invited to have tea with Mrs. Harry S. Truman, the President's wife. While they were drinking their tea, the President came into the room and sat down next to Grandma.

"You remind me of my mother," the President said. That was a great compliment, for Truman was very fond of his mother and often flew home to Missouri to visit her.

"Well," Grandma replied to the President, "you remind me of my sons." That was a great compliment too, for she loved her children.

The President had lived on a farm when he was a small boy. He and Grandma

discussed crops, livestock, and agriculture in general.

"You talk like a good farmer," Grandma said. "And I hear you are also a good piano player. Will you play something for me?"

"Why do you want to hear me play?" the President asked.

"So I can brag to all the people back home."

The President went to the piano and played Paderewski's *Minuet*. Grandma thanked him graciously.

When she returned to Eagle Bridge, the whole population turned out to welcome her home. All Grandma's neighbors were proud of their famous citizen who had won an award in Washington, and visited the First Lady and the President of the United States.

9. Grandma on TV

So many honors came to Grandma Moses that she could hardly accept them all. On her 90th birthday the mayor of Albany, the New York State capital, proclaimed "Grandma Moses Day."

Wearing a black jersey dress and a corsage of roses presented by one of her great-grandchildren, the famous painter arrived in Albany. Bells rang out "Happy Birthday," and she was given the keys to the city. She attended an exhibition of her paintings. Hundreds of people were there.

"I never knew I had so many friends," she said. That night Albany gave her a big birthday party. Her cake weighed 70 pounds and flamed with 90 candles.

"I feel no older than I did at seventy," she told the birthday guests.

"How are you going to celebrate your 100th birthday?" someone asked.

"I'm going to have a dance," Grandma Moses laughed. "I'll dance a jig. That's a promise."

A telegram arrived from President Truman. Grandma's heart warmed as she read, "May the spirit of spring and eternal sunshine be yours always."

Soon after her 90th birthday, she was proclaimed "Grandmother of the Nation" by some civic clubs.

"I have eleven grandchildren of my own," she joked, "seventeen great-grandchildren, and now I'm taking on one hundred and fifty million more grandchildren. I hope they don't all want Christmas presents."

In spite of all her honors, she kept right on working. She did most of her painting in her bedroom on a flat work table. She never used an easel.

Grandma Moses at work in 1955 in her Eagle Bridge home

Grandma started each day's painting early in the morning. Usually she worked on four pictures at a time.

"It saves paint," she explained. "I do the blue for one sky and then the other three skies. And I paint from the top down. First the sky, then the mountains, then the hills, then the trees, the houses, the cattle and the people."

There was a great deal of excitement at her house when a television crew arrived to film Grandma Moses with Ed Murrow for his *See It Now* series. After the film was made, it would be shown on the Columbia Broadcasting System network.

On the show Grandma Moses was as charming as her pictures.

"Anybody can paint," she said.

"I couldn't," Murrow protested.

"Oh, sure you could," Grandma said, handing him a paint brush. "Here, now, make a man."

Murrow said he couldn't even do that. He asked Grandma if she felt sorry when she saw one of her paintings sold.

"Of course not," she snapped. "I'd rather see the money." Now she appreciated the money her pictures made.

She told Murrow that she could remember the day Lincoln died. She talked about her own death, which she knew could come before long. "It will be like going to sleep," she said.

Many of her paintings were shown on the program, which was in color. All over America people saw the show and enjoyed it. "Grandma Moses was simply wonderful," *The New York Times* said.

But there was one person who didn't see the show, and that was Grandma herself. The night the film appeared on TV, the reception on her set was so bad that she turned it off and went to bed.

She wrote to the Columbia Broadcasting System and asked if there were any way for her to see the film. The company sent the film and a projector to Eagle Bridge.

The whole village turned out to see the film at the community center. Grandma Moses was escorted to a front seat. She wore a neat, black dress, a bright scarf, and a little pancake hat trimmed with roses.

The lights dimmed, and the film was flashed on the screen. "Oh, there I am," Grandma whispered. "Is that really me?"

When, on the film, she said that anyone could learn to paint, people sitting near her heard her whisper to herself. "Start with a tree, something simple, and keep on trying," she murmured. "One must never stop trying."

10. A Painting for a President

Grandma Moses had become America's favorite painter. Her paintings were reproduced on Christmas cards, and millions were sold throughout the world.

There was something about red barns, white steeples, and acres of snow that struck a responsive chord in the hearts of Americans. Perhaps it was a deep longing for the nation's simple past, which had long since disappeared.

Grandma Moses' paintings were reproduced on fabrics that were made into draperies, pillow cases, and upholstery. Her paintings were even reproduced on dinner plates. And at Dr. Kallir's suggestion she started painting tiles.

"It's like painting on marble," she said. "At first, I was disgusted. I couldn't use bright red or blue. . . . I was used to oils and the tile paints were a little like children's water colors. Once it's on, it's on for good. You can't make a mistake. You can't rub it out. But finally I got the hang of it."

Nearly all of these Grandma Moses products sold well. The checks that the painter received regularly became bigger and bigger. But Grandma never made much effort to sell her paintings.

Once she told a prospective customer to buy chickens instead. "Chickens can hatch more chickens," Grandma explained. "And besides, my pancakes are better than my paintings."

Grandma Moses was always ready to try something new. When Random House, a publishing company, asked her to illustrate a new edition of Clement C. Moore's *The Night Before Christmas*, Grandma Moses tackled the job with her usual confidence. Her pictures were so vivid and dramatic that they could be called poetry in paint.

Grandma Moses painted Santa's arrival for *The Night Before Christmas*.

President Dwight D. Eisenhower was a great admirer of her work. He liked to paint, too, and once sent Grandma Moses a reproduction of one of his pictures. "For Grandma Moses," he wrote, "a real artist, from a rank amateur."

The members of Eisenhower's cabinet asked Grandma Moses to paint a picture of the President's farm at Gettysburg, Pennsylvania. They wanted to give it to Eisenhower on the third anniversary of his inauguration.

Many photographs of his farm were sent to Grandma. She started working happily, using both the photographs and her own imagination.

The President had a small putting green for golf practice on his farm, and Grandma made it much larger than it really was. She also added a pony cart with the President's three grandchildren riding in it.

When the painting was finished, Grandma sent it to Washington with a note to the President that said, "I was very honored to be asked to paint a picture of your home in Gettysburg. Although most of my paintings are memories and imagination, I tried to do this for you and I hope it will please you."

Vice-President Richard Nixon unveiled the painting for the President at the White House. The President beamed with delight when he saw it. The next morning a picture of the painting appeared on the front pages of newspapers all over the United States. Grandma Moses was now more famous than ever.

11. One Hundred Years Young

As the 1950's drew to a close, Grandma Moses was living with her son Forrest and his wife, Mary, in a modern ranch house across the road from the old farmhouse where she had lived since 1905.

There were no stairs to climb in the new house, and Grandma was happy there. She rarely went outside, explaining, "I can't stay out in the sun anymore for I get freckles and they make me look kinda old."

Grandma Moses would be one hundred years old on September 7, 1960. As the magic date approached, her house swarmed with reporters and photographers.

"It's nothing to get that old," she told them, her eyes sparkling with laughter. "You just tell a lot of bad stories, you laugh, and you'll get there yourself. It's as easy as that.

"But I haven't got time to think about all the fuss. I've got too many things to occupy my mind. I've got to finish those paintings there on the couch and I've got lots of cards to sign." She gave a sly wink and added, "I've got lots of boy friends coming to see me. I don't show any partiality, because there'd be some black eyes if I did. But I've always said I'd dance a jig with Dr. Shaw on my 100th birthday."

A reporter asked if her eyesight was still good.

"Do you think I'd be painting if it were not?" she answered.

"Well," the reporter insisted, "is there anything wrong with you?"

"Nothing wrong with me except that I've got a broken neck," Grandma joked. "I got it from leaning over to sign so many checks."

Then she became more serious and said, "Painting is not important. The important thing is keeping busy."

A photographer got ready to take her picture. "Don't take me with my mouth open," she said. "Only trouble is, I can never keep it shut."

While she was talking, Dr. Shaw arrived. He felt her pulse.

"What about my broken neck?" Grandma

asked him with a grin. She turned to the reporters. "He never does anything about my neck. He won't believe I broke it. Well, I started to give him a spanking when he was a little kid, only I couldn't do it because his mother came along. But he's going to get it yet, just wait and see."

"She's a wonderful little old lady," Dr. Shaw said. "A very exquisite lady. And she's doing remarkably well. Grandma's tough. She's tough and she's hardy and she enjoys life."

Grandma decided to have a big birthday party on the Sunday before her actual birthday, so that members of her family who worked weekdays could come. Early that Sunday morning telegrams, flowers, people, and presents began to arrive for Grandma Moses.

A message from President Eisenhower said, "We have all benefited from your sense of the joy and beauty of life. Mrs. Eisenhower and I will always be especially grateful for your painting of our farm in Gettysburg."

There was an enormous birthday cake with 100 candles. Grandma asked some of her great-grandchildren to help blow them out.

Grandma Moses' great-grandchildren help her celebrate her 100th birthday.

"Wait!" one photographer cried. "We want to take your picture."

"If you were bright little girls and boys," Grandma said to the children, "you'd kick that cake right over and we could all have something to eat instead of sitting around waiting."

When the photographer was all ready, Grandma and the children gave a mighty puff, and all the candles went out.

"We blew them all out and we didn't even burn our noses," Grandma bragged.

As she greeted her guests, she held a bouquet in one hand. "This bouquet is because I'm one hundred," she said. "But I feel more like a bride. Well, now that I'm here the only thing to do is to go back to the beginning and start all over again. And that's exactly what I'm going to do."

On her real birthday three days after

the party, Dr. Shaw came to visit her.

"Come on, Dr. Shaw," Grandma said. "It's time for our dance."

"I'm too old to dance," Dr. Shaw objected.

"Why, you're just an eighty-four-year-old kid," Grandma said, pulling him to his feet.

Dr. Shaw took Grandma Moses in his arms, and they danced gaily around the room.

The next summer Grandma Moses had a bad fall, and Dr. Shaw sent her to a nursing home. She was still there on her 101st birthday.

"I'd like to hop, hop, hop around the room," she told her visitors. "I feel perfectly well. I ought to be up and about. My boards and brushes are waiting, but the doctor says I can't leave yet."

Grandma Moses never did leave the nursing home. She died quietly there on December 13, 1961.

"She just wore out," Dr. Shaw said.

Grandma Moses' life was finished, but not the final picture on which she had been working. Characteristically, it was called *Beautiful World*, and, like so many that she had completed, expressed the simple joys of life in the rural America of long ago.